Forklifts

Mari Bolte

CREATIVE EDUCATION • CREATIVE PAPERBACKS

seedlings

Published by Creative Education and Creative Paperbacks
P.O. Box 227, Mankato, Minnesota 56002
Creative Education and Creative Paperbacks
are imprints of The Creative Company
www.thecreativecompany.us

Design by Ellen Huber
Production by Alison Derry
Art direction by Tom Morgan

Photographs by Alamy (Chitsanupong Kathi, devilmaya), Getty (Danila Bolshakov/EyeEm, Kmatta, lingqi xie, Reza Estakhrian, Satakorn Sukontakajonkul/EyeEm, Sergey Dogadin, Yauhen Akulich), Shutterstock (BomMostFor, Chitsanupong Kathip, Dekliyngkaea, industryviews, Mirror-Images, Pissanu Jirakranjanakul, Shutter B Photo, Trovoboworod, Vereshchagin Dmitry)

Library of Congress Cataloging-in-Publication Data
Names: Bolte, Mari, author.
Title: Forklifts / Mari Bolte.
Other titles: Seedlings (Creative Education, Inc. (Mankato, Minn.))
Description: Mankato, Minnesota : Creative Education and Creative
    Paperbacks, [2024] | Series: Seedlings | Includes bibliographical
    references and index. | Audience: Ages 4–7 | Audience: Grades K–1 |
    Summary: "An early elementary-level STEM introduction to the forklift,
    covering how the construction vehicle looks and works. Includes a
    glossary, further resources, and a labeled image guide to the lifting
    machine's major parts"— Provided by publisher.
Identifiers: LCCN 2023012499 (print) | LCCN 2023012500 (ebook) | ISBN
    9781640269217 (library binding) | ISBN 9781682774717 (paperback) | ISBN
    9781640269996 (pdf)
Subjects: LCSH: Forklift trucks—Juvenile literature. | Construction
    equipment—Juvenile literature. | CYAC: Forklift trucks. | Construction
    equipment. | LCGFT: Instructional and educational works.
Classification: LCC TL296 .B65 2024 (print) | LCC TL296 (ebook) | DDC
    621.8/63—dc23/eng/20230331
LC record available at https://lccn.loc.gov/2023012499
LC ebook record available at https://lccn.loc.gov/2023012500

Printed in China

TABLE OF CONTENTS

Time to Lift! 4

Small Machines 6

Fierce Forks 8

On the Job 10

Heavy Loads 12

The Wheels' Job 14

Mighty Machine 16

All Done Lifting! 18

Picture a Forklift 20

Words to Know 22

Read More 23

Websites 23

Index 24

Time to lift!

Forklifts are small machines. They lift and move things from place to place.

Forklifts have two forks on the front. The forks go up and down. They slide under a load. Then they lift it.

9

Forklifts move supplies. They stack boxes in warehouses. These boxes are often on pallets.

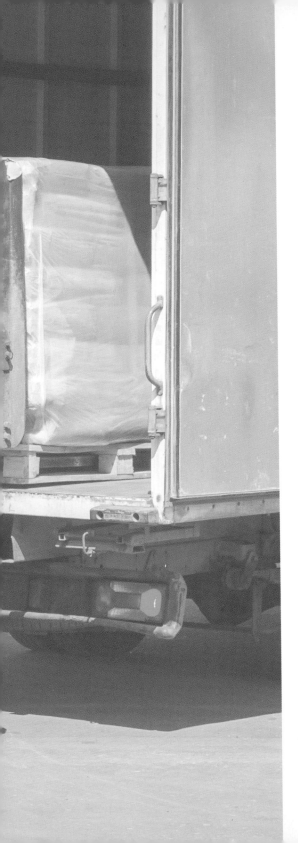

Counterweights are on the back of a forklift. They keep it from tipping over. Forklifts can carry very heavy loads.

Forklifts have
four wheels.
The front
wheels help
hold the load.

The back wheels steer.

Some forklifts move barrels. Some move rolls of paper. Others lift workers high in the air!

All done lifting!

Picture a Forklift

mast

forks

cab

counterweight

wheels

counterweight: an added weight that helps balance a load

fork: a long, strong prong

pallet: a platform (usually of wood) for storing and handling goods

warehouse: a place to store goods

Read More

Bolte, Mari. *Wheel Loaders*. Mankato, Minn.: Creative Education and Creative Paperbacks, 2024.

Harasymiw, Luke. *Forklifts*. New York: Gareth Stevens Publishing, 2020.

Websites

Forklift Facts for Kids
https://kids.kiddle.co/Forklift
Learn about forklifts and what they do.

Materials Handling
https://kids.britannica.com/students/article/materials-handling/275732
Read about the role forklifts play in making things.

Index

barrels, **17**
boxes, **10**
counterweights, **13**
forks, **8**
pallets, **10**
steering, **15**
supplies, **10**
warehouses, **10**
wheels, **14, 15**
workers, **17**